From the Beginning Until Now

Ann B. Rhodes

Copyright © 2016 by Ann B. Rhodes

All rights reserved. No part of this publication may be reproduced, distributed, or transmitted in any form or by any means, including photocopying, recording, or other electronic or mechanical methods, without the prior written permission of the publisher, except in the case of brief quotations embodied in critical reviews and certain other noncommercial uses permitted by copyright law. For permission requests, write to the publisher, addressed "Attention: Permissions Coordinator," at the address below.

Ann B. Rhodes
Email address: Smilingannie923@yahoo.com

ISBN: 978-1-62217-789-9

Dedication

This book is dedicated to my mother, Alma Rhodes, for always believing in me; my niece, Tianna Rhodes; my nephew, Malcolm; and my two brothers, Bennie, Jr. and Roy.

Contents

Section 1: Life, What a Wonderful Gift to Have!

What is Life? 1
Life 2
It's a Part of Life 3

Section 2: Special Days

December 5
The Greatest Easter Gift 6
What is a Mother? 7

Section 3: People Who Have Made A Difference

A Great Man 9
I Will Always Remember You 10
I Will Remember You Always 13
To a Friend I Will Remember Always 15
Mr. Pflueger 16
Mr. Wearden 17
She Was Like a Grandmother to Me 18

Section 4: A Spiritual Atmosphere

Thank You, Jesus 20
Praise God 21
Well, I Will Continue to Pray 22
Getting Saved 24
The Way I Make It Through 26

JEALOUSY	27
ENCOURAGEMENT	28
MAKING A CHANGE	29
SURVIVING	30
MY GOD SHALL SUPPLY MY NEEDS	32
CHURCH	33
WALK AWAY	34
DEAR LORD	35
MY PATH TO A NEW BEGINNING	36
A SOLDIER'S RETURN	38

SECTION 5: PRAYERS

A STUDY PRAYER	40
A TRAVELING PRAYER	41
MARRIAGE PRAYER	43

SECTION 6: MEMORIES

MY FIRST YEAR OF TEACHING	45
IT SEEMS LIKE JUST YESTERDAY	47
SAYING GOOD-BYE TO A SCHOOL	49
ITS LAST DAYS	51
FAREWELL	52
SCHOOL YEARS	53

SECTION 7: MY OTHER POEMS

FRESHMAN IN HIGH SCHOOL	55
TO BE A TEACHER	58
WHAT IS GOSSIP?	60
PLEASE, STOP THE VIOLENCE	62
THE POINT OF VIEW IN MY EYES	64

If She Only Knew 65
Being Unique 67
Save It Until Marriage 68
Facing Only the Facts 69
Mommy, You're Always Right 71
Hard Decisions 73
What is Happiness? 75
An Angel 76
A Teacher Retiree 77
Crying Unto Jesus 79
Facing My Reality 80
A Mother... 82

Section I

Life,
What a Wonderful Gift to Have!

What is Life?

What is life?
I was asked one day.
I didn't know the answer,
so what could I say.

Life is a door.
It has opportunities that can open and close in your face,
and if you believe in your dreams,
you can change anything that comes along the way.

Life is a lightning bolt.
It can flash before your eyes.
You can have happiness and heartbreak
along with a lot of cries.

Life is like a cake,
only if you use the best ingredients,
by showing people love, honor, and respect,
but most of all being obedient.

What is life?
I was asked one day.
It is a beautiful gift from God
that will not last always.

LIFE

Life is a long adventurous journey
that contains many bumpy roads to travel on,
but as long as you have God on your side
you will not travel on that road alone.

As you travel on these bumpy roads
you can allow them to tear your life apart,
or let it be the beginning
of a new start in life.

As the wind blows harder and harder
and the sirens begin to sound,
you realize that life is a special gift
and that our time on Earth is winding down.

As the angels from heaven come
and whisper, "Come with me to a better place,"
your life flashes before your eyes
and *Amazing Grace* begins to play.

When your journey called life is complete,
you drop down on your knees to say good-bye,
 and thank God for this beautiful gift
and pray to cross those pearly gates
to see your family again.

It's a Part of Life

Life is rough like sandpaper.
It can also be as sweet as a piece of candy,
like a Reese's, Twix, or a pack of M&M's,
but at times it is bittersweet like a sour piece of candy.

It reminds me of a Warheads that has an instant sour taste, but as it is
in your mouth for a while
the taste will slowly get better.

Life is like a seesaw.
It has a lot of ups and downs.
Everyone has his or her own problems,
but a positive attitude can always make things turn around.

Life is like a camera flash.
It's quick, and a change can occur in an instant.
 The change can be a positive opportunity
or a devastating tragedy.

Life is similar to a butterfly,
because things can easily slip away.
You can give up your dreams and opportunities
that you will never see again.

Life is like a flower getting ready to blossom,
or someone trying to scare you at night.

But remember things happen for a reason,
and it is all a part of life.

ANN B. RHODES

Section 2

Special Days

December

December is the last month
that ends this year.
The weather changes from warm like a cup of hot chocolate
to being so cold that ice and frost are on cars each morning.

The wind starts howling like a wolf
that tells you to make sure that you have socks, hats, and a big coat.
Sometimes snow may fall quickly
like balls of cotton coming out of the sky,
and you will see children making snowmen with their hats and gloves on.

Some children throw snowballs at each other
to make each feel freezing cold,
while others go skiing down
and cross high slopes.

Finally, people shop for different kinds of gifts
for the last holiday of the year,
to bring lots of joy and happiness
to their wonderful family and friends.

The Greatest Easter Gift

When spring comes in April,
it brings strong blowing winds.
Outside, children play tag or red rover or hide-and-seek,
for school is out for a week.

As they play, the wind gets colder and colder,
pushing them back inside for their coats and gloves,
or to sit by the fire.

Inside, after they've warmed,
they jump in delight
as the girls receive their Easter dresses
and the boys their Easter baskets.

A friend sits down beside the children in the living room
to tell them the story of the greatest Easter gift:
"Easter comes once a year
during the cold of March or April,
but we take time to worship Jesus Christ
the man who bore the cross.

"He died for the love of every skin color and nationality,
but on Easter Sunday arose reborn,
having paid for the world's sin."

We must lift our hands high or put them together in prayer.
We must talk to Jesus Christ, telling him,
"When you died on the cross and arose,
you bestowed on all of God's children
the greatest Easter gift."

What is a Mother?

(Dedicated to my loving mother, Mrs. Alma Rhodes.)

What is a mother?
A mother is a heart pumping love.
Mine opened her arms to enfold me,
she bent over like a maple,
a shield from the torrents and the blistering sun.

My mother opened herself like a book
in which she had written, "Go, child, and do."
She let me soar from that page like Noah's spring-bearing dove.
She gave me myself.

Section 3

People Who Have Made a Difference

A Great Man

(Dedicated to Dr. Shields Upchurch, assistant principal at Callaway High School, during his retirement in May 2004.)

During my four long years of high school,
I had a rigorous and dark journey to complete.
Besides the heartwarming words from my mother,
there was always a generous man who helped me.

Math was like a foreign language,
with many formulas as hard as the rocks outside.
This noble man always made me do two things:
First, explain to him what he just said,
Second, answer the question, "Why?"

His watchful eyes scanned my essays for grammatical errors,
and he rebuked me if I submitted them late,
but no matter what he might be doing
he always stopped to help.

So today I thank a great man
who gave me a helping hand,
and who taught me this essential lesson:
"I must never say, 'I can't,'
because I always know I can."

I Will Always Remember You

(Dedicated to Russell Wearden, my middle school science teacher.)

I close my eyes to view the camera inside my head.
The video takes me back to my adolescent years.

I smile as I remember my middle school science teacher.
As this tape begins to rewind inside my head,
I remember the different lessons my science teacher taught me
and the ideas of mine that he praised.

One lesson that I have learned,
and it's something that my mother says to me every day,
"You can do wrong things for a long time,
but soon it will catch up with you
and you will reap what you sow."

I still remember all of the gossip from that time period,
and all of the malicious things that I had said,
but this situation made me realize
that I hurt someone that I deeply respected.

Every time I made a mistake
I see a note that has an important message.
This message gave me something to think about.

I try to fast forward through
all the terrible mistakes that I made.

You were one of the teachers who was always there for me.

It took me two years to realize
the message that you were trying to get across,
but now that I understand that message well,
I will listen to the truth and not the falsehood.

As I pray to God
and I list all my plans and goals in a journal.
I will always remember a teacher
who sometimes acted like a dad.

As I move up one step higher on the mountain,
and climb this mountain higher and higher each day,
I am developing stronger character
and becoming a leader who will be as solid as a rock.

Next year I will not be in middle school,
I will be in a building that's up the hill
containing more bricks.
I will have a different science teacher,
still remembering all the crazy jokes and laughs.

I will always find the tape that contains the memories
and the kind words that you have brought into my life,
the times that you had to correct me as a student
and the lessons that you had taught.

I have said it all the year
I have not done it one time yet,
but now, as I get to do that one thing,
I am now finally realizing what I meant.

ANN B. RHODES

As I am promoted up to ninth grade,
I will remember at least one thing that you taught,
but now as I said during the year,
"I am finally going off" into my second adventure of educational endeavors.

I Will Remember You Always

(Dedicated to Judy Yonce, an exemplary teacher.)

As I sit in my favorite chair in my room,
I daydream back to my years in middle and high school,
and my memory brings me back to a teacher
who always traveled with me along the way.

You appeared like an angel with your wings open
during my seventh grade year.
I had a flashback of taking Algebra I in eighth grade
from a different teacher.
Mrs. Yonce, without your clever hints
this class wasn't fun.

I remember taking geometry,
learning about different shapes and proofs,
but all that year I said,
"I can never find another teacher like you."

My tenth grade year taking Algebra II was wonderful.
You wrote the objectives on the overhead
so all of your students could understand the lesson.
You made me realize during my junior year that
math was my best subject
as long as I continued to read.

It has taken me four years to realize
that math is not as hard as I thought.
Lots of hard work and dedication
brought me through what you taught.

As I look back over those days
and as I approached my senior year,
I thank the Lord up above
that I had a teacher like you.

You have always inspired me,
and encouraged me throughout the years,
to always do my best
so I will shine above the rest.

You are that one special teacher
who went that extra mile,
to help me see the way
through my hard times with a smile.

You are that one special teacher
who always helped a student overcome a difficult obstacle.
Just remember as you move,
how deeply *that hurt me* too!

To a Friend I Will Remember Always

(Dedicated to Jamie Smith, my saxophone partner in middle school.)

I can always think of one person
who stood by me and was a true friend.
I have all the memories
of different places we have been together
flashing back in my mind.
Our friendship began when we were ten years old.

There was a time
when we didn't know each other's name,
but you were always the person
that came to the rescue.

As my mind imagines the future
and the goals that I have in life,
I will always remember a friend
who was a strong leader for me.

Next year we will go our separate ways,
but we will still be in the same state.
The time has come now
for some words that I really didn't want to say,
"Good-bye to my best friend,
who I shall remember always."

Mr. Pflueger

(Dedicated to my middle school band director.)

I know a person
whose name is Mr. Pflueger.
Isn't that a weird name to pass on to one of your children?

He tries to act funny
like another teacher that I know.
When he plays basketball,
he acts like a professional.
When he smiles at you,
you can smile back at him.

He looks very young
for his age.
If you act like an ape,
He will go on a rampage.

He likes to play the drums.
That's his favorite instrument.
He once drove a black truck
with the windows tinted.

He makes a long-winded speech
when you can't play a song,
Don't make him mad
because he'll change his tone.

He gets real red
when he gets real mad.
When he's by himself,
he sings Popeye the Sailorman.

Mr. Wearden

Mr. Wearden was my science teacher,
crazy as he could be.
He drove a little truck,
and as his eyes looked at you,
you know there was a mystery.

He taught me for four years,
I enjoyed being in his class,
science was a subject I didn't like,
but with him, I got a lot of laughs.

He has a wife and two daughters,
he's even a preacher, too.
It took his students a long time to believe him.

He can be strict and very honest,
he can be as quiet as a bee,
he can daydream in wonderland,
and then can return back in a flash.

Where does he get his name from?
I don't have any idea.
One thing I wanted to say,
"Mr. Wearden, way to go in your years of being an educator!"

She Was Like a Grandmother to Me

(In memory of the late Mrs. Margaret Talley Johnson.)

I have a picture of your face,
and I can only hold onto the memories inside of my head.

You have paid the debt that we all have to pay one day.
I see a sign coming from the Lord
that our time to be with the Lord, like you, isn't far away.

When I reflect back on the past,
I remember all the joyful and sad memories.

I have to ask,
"Are you really gone?
or are you just away?"
because we will meet again in eternal life one day.

I don't have anything but a picture
to cherish your everlasting memory forever and always.

They say that everything happens for a reason,
though I often wonder why.
Should I hold back these drenching tears,
or let them loose and attack my cry?

I see no evil, I fear no evil, of the Lord when he comes my way.
I hope you're "Resting in Peace"
because you were like a grandmother to me.

SECTION 4

A SPIRITUAL ATMOSPHERE

Thank You, Jesus

When I was worried about an unbearable situation,
my mother told me to pray about it because Jesus will always be there.

At first I cried
And asked the Lord to guide me.

"Father, please lead me and run all this evil away.
Lord, I ask that you forgive me because if I have faith, you have the power, my Lord.

God, I thank you for the blessings that you have given me,
because without you, my Lord, I would not have accomplished anything.

Sometimes I just wanted to give up,
but my mother told me to let Jesus handle it, and he came through.

I hear and see no evil
because the Lord is my light and salvation, and I will fear no one.

Father, I thank you and ask that you guide my way
so I can continue to walk in your light and prosper along the way."

Praise God

As I wake up in the morning,
I say, "Thank you, Jesus Christ,"
Thank you my Lord, my Savior,
for waking me again.

I say unto thee,
"The Lord is the head of my life,
for I walk by the love of faith
and not by the love of sight".

I thank you, Jesus Christ,
for another glorious day.
I can never thank God enough,
for he shows me and guides the way.

The Lord is my Shepherd,
I shall not want for anything.
No food, no glass, no tea.

I can do all things through Christ,
for he strengthens me every day.
If it is God's will for me to do,
I shall do as he will say.

As I fall asleep at night,
I ask God to wash my sins away,
that I shall be made whole and purified
in the name of the Father, the Son, and the Holy Ghost.

ANN B. RHODES

Well, I Will Continue to Pray

I woke up early one morning
and I began to cry,
asking the Lord up above,
"Why? Why is there so much jealousy and hurt in the world?
Is this something that we must all go through?
Is this something that we all deserve?"

I pray and ask God sometimes,
"Why does life have to be this way?
Will I wake up one morning and it will be a whole new day?"

I have always said to myself
that everything happens for a reason,
then the Lord calls his roll for someone to come home
and never to return.

I ask the Lord to guide me
and lead me in that special way,
so maybe sometime soon
I will have a prosperous new day.

My mother has always taught me
that you must begin as a child
to build your empire in life,
so when you get older you will see how you have triumphed through
the tough aspects of life.

I have a dream like Dr. Martin Luther King, Jr. did one day.
I will make this world a better place
and have a new season like Accent and seasoning salt.

Children should be encouraged more in school,
instead of acting out for the attention they don't receive at home.

Well, I will continue to pray
that my life will have a brighter day like the sunshine outside,
And before I die,
my soul will go to the heavens and the dusts of the earth.

Getting Saved

An angel came down from heaven
praying on her hands and knees,
begging me to change my life
by saying, "Jesus is what I need."

In the beginning I was scared
and worried where my soul might go.
Hopefully, it will go to heaven,
but then it may go to hell, who knows?

This angel came down and spoke to me
and said, "Change your wicked ways!"
Do you want to live through Christ, or shorten your days?"
I fell down on my knees and began to pray,
and then a white light flashed before my eyes.
It was the spirit of Jesus to guide
and show me where my heart was true.

God is teaching me a lesson
and wants me to make the right decision,
to be a role model for others
in the mysterious land of the living.

I have learned a lot of things
for the twenty plus years of my life,
but God has put me through a lot
so I can put up a strong fight.

After my uncle died, I finally made the decision
of where I want to go in life,
and that is to accept Jesus, repent for my sins,
and have everlasting life.

The Way I Make It Through

The way I make it through
is by the will and the grace of God.
I pray for the Lord to guide me
so I can reach for the stars.

Sometimes the path I travel on
is a tough one I have to face,
but nothing is really hard
as long as I have God here running my race.

I must look to the Lord and thank him,
and praise him for his name,
for the things he has done for me
and how he has guided me through the way.

I know I am not the best person or child in the world,
but I am a special someone
that I can do all things through the Lord.

Lord, I ask you to forgive me
as I repent for my sins,
because the devil cannot interfere with me,
he can only lose and not win.

Your guardian angel stands beside me
and protects me from whatever the devil tries to do,
because I pray and ask for your guidance
and that's the way I make it through.

Jealousy

We grow up in a society
full of anger, jealousy, and hate,
but the Bible says, "Love all your enemies,"
and follow that "Christian way."

People are always jealous
no matter what you try to do.
Make good grades on a test
and they say, "You must have cheated,"
not even did your best.

I always try to wonder
what makes people go that evil way,
but that's a question unanswered
that God will have to answer one day.

God doesn't allow jealousy in his kingdom,
nor does he allow a grudge,
because to him everyone is equal.

Jealousy of your skin color
and the clothes and styles you wear,
but it's like the Lord said,
"He will not put on you
any more than you can bear."

If there's anytime you have a problem
with the jealousy that's going around,
give it to the hands of God
and he will fight your battle to the ground.

Encouragement

A hummingbird has landed,
but must move away,
and refuses to get up
then changes his mind.

The hummingbird gives up hope
as a guardian angel comes by
to give the bird strength
and encourages the bird to fly.

This encouragement gives the bird peace
of mind along with his spirit and soul,
so he could one day be united as a whole.

The guardian angel teaches the hummingbird to live and fight for what
he may lose.
Encouragement gives the hummingbird power
and the courage to go home
and to sing an inspirational song
on his journey to see his family again.

Making a Change

A new year, a new millennium,
is coming on its way,
but I know for some people
it will just be another day.

I was born in the 1900s,
in the 80s to be exact,
but the year 2000 is approaching
and I know I need to change.

Will I change my ways
And go in the right path?
To talk to God and ask him
to forgive me for what I have done?

I'm in college now
and I want to have a successful life,
change and devote my life to God
because I know that's the way that's right.

The car accident I was involved in was a lesson,
not a mistake,
to warn me of my ways
that if I don't change, and soon,
I will encounter an early grave.

Surviving

I examine my life,
then I look at myself
wondering and asking the question,
"Does my life really need help?"

I try to imagine myself
 about five years from now,
but sometimes I look at my trials and tribulations
and ask, "How?"

How can I achieve wonderful accomplishments
that I should be proud of?
And only receive them
from the Lord up above.

I ask myself, "How did I get this way?"
but more importantly, "How can I change?"
So I will change and travel in the right direction
and have some better days.

The time has come now
to be the Ann I was once long ago,
and stop my mischief and madness
and develop a new soul,
develop a new spirituality,
and a new personal thought
with love, peace, happiness,
and care that comes from within the heart and soul.

As I explore my journey of life,
I need to be careful and make no mistakes,
but through it all
I am brave, bold, and intelligent,
and yes, I will survive.

My God Shall Supply My Needs

As I lay my head down, down to sleep,
I pray to the Lord, "My soul he shall keep."
I ask him to guide me, and show me the way,
So peace, joy, and happiness will be my amazing grace.

Whenever times are tough
and the devil steps in my way,
I pray to the Lord for guidance
and protection from evil things.

Sometimes I want to quit
and say, "Lord, just take me away,"
but a guardian angel from heaven
comes to show me my better days.

How times have been good
and the goals I have achieved,
and by keeping two words close to my heart
and that is saying, "I believe."

A preacher told me once
that my faith will carry me a long way
as long as hope is my spiritual leader
and my path for eternity.

Church

We should come to church to praise the Lord
whether it's day or night, Sunday, or a day during the week.
Most people come early in the morning to worship God.

We learn about God
in many different ways.
We can read our Holy Bible, attend Bible study and Sunday school, or
just listen to what the preacher has to say.

Church is a place
to come to on Sundays mornings
to hear some new things about God
so you can receive your spiritual food for nourishment.
Always get down on your hands and knees to pray for yourself and others.

Don't come to church to see who came to the service for that day,
or to see what the other members were wearing,
or just to come.
Always come to church to become closer in the spirit to God
and fill yourself up with plentiful nourishment.

Walk Away

If a bully says something to you
and tries to start to a fight,
look to the Lord and ask him,
"Will you guide me and be my light?"

If a person says a statement
and wants you to be mad,
have a smile and kill them with kindness.
When you think about it, you will be glad.

If this has been going on for years
and you see that there is no hope,
ask yourself this one question,
"Is it really his or her level I want to go?"

If what I said won't help you,
you'll have to handle it the old-fashioned way,
because God will take it into consideration
when it becomes Judgment Day.

Dear Lord

Dear Lord,
Father, I come before you today
to pray a special prayer.
One prayer is for my mom,
one prayer is for myself.

Father, as I pray
I want you to guide me to the light.
I know that miracles can happen,
because I walk by faith
and not by sight.

Lord, I prayed unto you
that you changed me and you did.
I know if I ask you for forgiveness,
you will forgive me for my sins.

Thank you, Lord, for being there by my side.

My Path to a New Beginning

The preacher and the ushers opened up the doors to the church.
There sat a chair on both sides of the aisle.
I had been attending this church for years,
 but I never became a member.

The spirit of the Lord whispered in my ear,
"Go confess your life unto God."
I walked down the aisle from the back row
and everyone continued singing.
The Lord put upon my heart to join the church.

Myself, along with some others,
attended classes with the pastor and assistant pastor
to understand the true meaning of joining the church
and being baptized.

During the class, I learned that baptism
stands for the death, burial, and resurrection of Jesus Christ.

God had truly been working with me for a long time.
I just had to take action and do something about it.

Baptism day had come
and there was a mini church service held
for all the people who were getting baptized.

I had always been scared of water, and in my mind I thought,
"What am I doing? I can't swim."

Before I left home, my mom said,
"If you are scared to be baptized,
you are scared of Jesus."

I believe that I was the third person to get baptized.
I walked down into the pool of the church.
I have no remembrance of what the preacher said.
I held my breath,
he took me under the water,
and he brought me back up, and I was still breathing.

It was not as bad as I thought,
but I did feel better about myself
because I know I encountered the death, burial, and resurrection through Christ.
I will now begin a new path in life to a new beginning.

A Soldier's Return

(In memory of my cousin, Ricky Hardaway, and my uncles, Luther Hardaway, Joe Henry Hardaway, Jr., and Henry Elmer Hardaway.)

The soldier closes his eyes and goes into a deep sleep
because the road he traveled on was rough like a rock.
God found him a smoother road.

This road contains a barrel full of roses that shows God's love,
 because his soldier wants to return home.
His journey begins during the darkness of the night
as he awakes from his sleep.
He notices he is on the other side of the mountain.

A light shines, the wind blows,
and God appears with an angel wearing golden wings.

He says to his soldier,
"You are now standing by a rainbow that has gold
for all the riches you never had.
Your new home has no cracks or holes of pain.
Rest in peace my soldier, welcome home."

SECTION 5

PRAYERS

A Study Prayer

My eyes are open wide to pray
before my head lays down to sleep.
I kneel with my hands together
in prayer that God will guide me.

"Dear God,
Direct me like an eagle soaring in the sky,
through the clouds filled with rain, so that I can see through the fog,
and through the path of any test,
anything else I should do
so I will be a glowing star.

Protect me like a soldier with a shield everywhere I stand,
and let an angel fly down from heaven
to give me the tree full of knowledge
so I will do my best.

My eyes are weary
after hours of pages turning and writing notes,
but, Lord, shine the light on me
so I know the trail of how to complete my path.

Thank you for walking by my side
and putting your hands inside of mine
during this prayer, because
I am covered with that blanket of encouragement
and believe 'I can do all things
through Christ which strengthens me.'"

Amen

A Traveling Prayer

(Dedicated to all Hillcrest Elementary staff members transferring to Franklin Forest Elementary for 2005-06.)

My eyes are open wide to pray
before my head lays down to sleep.
I kneel with my hands together
in prayer that God will guide me.

"Dear God,
Direct me like an eagle soaring in the sky
through this new path
and test of change
so I will be a glowing star.

Protect me like a soldier,
and let an angel fly down from heaven
to provide me with the tree of knowledge
so I will do my best and survive the challenges of change.

My eyes have become weary
after hours of packing and moving boxes,
preparing to travel from one home to the new one,
but Lord, shine a bright light near me
so I know the trail to follow in the path of my new home.

Thank you for walking by my side
and putting your hands inside of mine
during this transitioning time that struck like a bolt of lightning.

I am covered with a warm blanket of encouragement,
full of the memories and experiences that I have captured with the flashing camera inside
my head.

Regardless of where I may be or who I work around,
I will always remember that I can do all things through Christ,
because he is the spirit who strengthens me
into a stronger individual."

Amen

Marriage Prayer

Lord, I want to thank you
as I bend my knees to pray,
that I may keep this promise that I made to my companion
until death may take me away.

My life is now connected to someone
who shares the same love as I do for Jesus.

Father, bless this holy bond of matrimony
that we shall be united together as a whole
and share a bundle of love for each other.

Lord, just bless my family
and all our happiness that will continue
during all our journeys along the way.

Amen

Section 6

Memories

My First Year of Teaching

"Five, four, three, two, one,"
I count down the days
until I can arrange my classroom.

I walk into an improvised room
that has two cabinets, a sink,
and lots of furniture,
but using my mind's eye
I organize a room with a welcoming aspect.

Days before the students enter,
I receive a collection of notebooks
and a mountain of paperwork
that will keep me occupied all year.

The principal and the instructional specialist
give me supplies for a challenging nine months.
I receive a clock, a stapler,
a box of tissue, Tylenol, and a set of business cards.

A rainbow of students enter as quietly as mice
and search for their desks.
During the first weeks,
they familiarize themselves with school rules
and practice procedures until they become routine.

Some days shine as bright as the sun,
while others twist and turn around me like tornadoes,
and the students themselves like dervishes.

At the year's end, full of energy,
they rumble like elephants through every task,
but with a glint in their eyes
hinting at their readiness
for next year's trek across the savannahs of learning.

It Seems Like Just Yesterday

It seems like just yesterday
I was born into a world full of people of many colors
and noises that made me cry.
It made my eyes turn red and my head started throbbing with pain,
like a band member beating on drums.

It seems like just yesterday
I was in a kindergarten class filled
with many colorful bulletin board displays
and music that I could sing along with all day.

Then the teenage years came knocking on the door,
bringing me the silver keys to a car.
This car brought me a long journey
of traveling down several roads to find a job.

The job I found was filled with several voices, scanning, and bagging groceries
with a salary of only minimum wage.

It seems like just yesterday
it was a rainy January afternoon
as my mother and I traveled on the interstate to the hospital
to wait for the arrival of my niece to be born into a new world.

She was so scared, because she started looking around the hospital room and crying.

It seems like just yesterday
I was a senior in high school,
waiting to march across the stage in the auditorium
to receive my diploma,
as I listened to *Pomp and Circumstance*.

There's one important message that I would like to say to each graduating class,
"Always stand up tall with your head held high in the air,
believe in your hopes and dreams,
and always bow down on your knees to pray,
because when you finally complete your hopes and dreams,
it will seem like it happened yesterday."

Saying Good-bye to a School

(In Memory of Hogansville High School)

It's so hard to say good-bye
to a school you could call your own.
It's hard to believe this next year
the Greenwave will be gone.

Walking down the halls,
I remember hearing, "Hey you, my friend."
Everyone had a smiling face
in a friendly place.

When something happened,
everyone was concerned.
Knowing all the teachers,
students knew with who to share their thoughts.

Our community came together
when our middle grades' building passed away.
Even the student body remembered it for years.

The first recommendation of the consolidation with Troup County
began when I was an elementary student.
At first it was rejected
and the issue ended for a couple of years.

Troup County suggested the consolidation again,
this time it was successful.
The smiles and frowns on faces
understood the beginning of change.

If we look at yesterday, and what tomorrow brings,
the colors of crimson and black
replace the white and green.

Although Hogansville High was in an unfamiliar town,
the Greenwave winning the championship
let us know for next year,
we'll also be losing a home.

When we move to Callaway Middle/High School,
we'll have a larger campus in a different location
and encounter many challenges.

As the doors of Hogansville High
get ready to close and open up,
we pass it down to the elementary children in a building where we left off.

The beginning of another school year
means walking into another home,
remembering that the Greenwave will last always.

It's so hard to say good-bye,
to a school you could call your own,
we leave with our Greenwave memories
locked in our hearts and in our souls.

Its Last Days

(In memory of Hogansville High School closing in 1996.)

The week had finally arrived
for everyone to say, "Good-bye,"
and walk the halls and classrooms
the last time we could call our school Hogansville High.

The tradition of the Greenwave would always be in our hearts,
because Hogansville High will always be our home.

The student council organized a time capsule ceremony
for faculty, staff, and students to put money, poems, and notes inside of it,
so one day someone will remember the closing of an era.

Although we must think about the future and not the past,
we will have the memories a school like this has had.

The school year went by quickly,
and it was honored in many ways,
but truly all the students who attended Hogansville High School
"saved the best for last."

Farewell

(This poem is also dedicated to the faculty and staff transferring from Hillcrest Elementary to Franklin Forest Elementary.)

The time has finally come
for us to travel our separate ways,
and say our final good-bye
as some of us move into a new place.

We have had some wonderful chats together,
watching the students at Hillcrest grow.
We move on to the different challenges
and many obstacles we have to face.

Change is hard like a rock
that often brings tears to our eyes,
but we need to reflect back on our joyful memories
as we say our last good-bye.

Best wishes to you all
as this school year finally comes to an end.
Let's look forward to new developments with bright sunshine ahead of us
as our new adventures are filled with new faces and experiences, and
movement in education begins.

School Years

When the school year begins in August,
students have to attend school for 180 days
to be taught math, English, reading, writing, science, and social studies,
and participate in the favorite class, PE.

A toddler begins with preschool,
learning those ABC's
Pre-K teachers teach students how to follow the rules,
and reward good behavior with a treat.

Then it's on to elementary school,
and students have a break called recess.
In the first to fifth grades,
students prepare early for high scores on the Georgia Criterion Referenced Competency Test.
(Now it's called Georgia Milestones Assessment System – GMAS.)

Next, you travel to middle school,
being in grades six to eight.
As the subjects get harder and harder,
students learn different ways to procrastinate.

Finally, it's on to high school,
with the completion of four more years,
but the only way to get out of high school
is to pass the Georgia High School Graduation exam.
(Now End of Course Test –ECOT.)

Students have a choice to go to college or technical school,
and graduate with a diploma or degree,
and have the job they really want,
while some students have to pay back those tuition fees.

I have always heard one say
that a mind is a terrible thing to waste,
because without a valuable education,
life will be even harder to face.

Freshman in High School

The first year of high school
is a challenge we all have to face
no matter how tall or short you are,
or your religion or your race.

You have to start taking different courses,
and you have to earn credit for every class.
Even if you don't like the subject,
love it anyway so you will pass the course.

In high school it's so different,
because you have to take final exams.
My only advice to you
is to get plenty of prayer and rest.

Another difference in high school
is that if you miss too many days,
you'll have to take that class again,
studying the same thing,
possibly from the same teacher.

Math is a little harder
beginning with Algebra I.
You can make the class tough
or you can make it a lot of fun.

When you think about quitting school,
remember you only have three more years to go.
Do you want your high school diploma?
It's a simple question to answer yes or no.

One good thing about being in high school
is that they have a name for every grade.
If you can make it through your freshman year,
the next three years will be a piece of cake.

Section 7

My Other Poems

To be a Teacher

To be a teacher,
I am a mother
who values every student.
I will provide a literature-rich environment
that has many books from a variety of cultures.

To be a teacher,
I am a singer
who sings my class a song,
greets them in the morning,
and says "Good-bye" to them before they go home.

To be a teacher,
I am an instructor
who provides my students with learning strategies,
so that their knowledge inside their brain will always increase.

To be a teacher,
I am a manager
who has a plan for every classroom session.
My students will know the consequences
for breaking any rule.

To be a teacher,
I am a participant
who does the hands-on activities that my students do, so that I can authentically assess their progress.

To be a teacher,
 I am a mentor
who pats them on the back and says "Good job!" for them to do their best,
so as they become older
they will outshine the rest.

To be a teacher,
I am a model
who has an important goal,
to challenge the mind of all of my students
while I inspire them to continue to be the best that they can be.

What is Gossip?

What is gossip?
I was asked one day.
I knew what it was,
but what could I say?

It is lies and spreading rumors.
It is as quiet as it can be.
It is lollygagging in the halls,
or a blind man that could see.

It's as quick as a bullet.
It's as sly as a dog.
Sometimes it wants to be stopped,
but it dares to stand alone.

It is hurtful and harmful.
It is as mean as it can be.
It is being very loquacious,
or as ripe as a peach.

It is being nasty and cheating.
It is being rude with delight.
It knows it is causing trouble,
and tries to start a fight.

It is being crazy and foolish.
It is being full of hate and deceit.
It is getting mad if you don't win,
and your heart is full of defeat.

What is gossip?
I was asked one day.
It is lies and being hurtful toward others,
so don't dare step in its way.

Please, Stop the Violence

I open my eyes
in a world filled with sounds, such as pop, bang, and slap.
Violence is our number one problem
that seems to be taking our lives away.

I drive around the city I live in,
then I sit down in my chair to watch the news.
My heart drops to the floor when I hear
"John Doe was shot last night."

My mind wonders,
"How could someone take another life?"
I look up at the ceiling to say,
"God, I want to first pray for the parents
so they can have a closer relationship to their child.
I hope that they showed their child the unconditional love they needed,
and not the bitter hatred that so many children have to encounter."

Some researchers and educators blame everything on television,
but I challenge you to answer this question,
"Is television the reality of all this violence?"

As our society ponders
on ways to unite to stop all the violence,
we must first come together as a community
to continue this STOP THE VIOLENCE campaign.
Start with the young generation
because if we start with them,
maybe one or a couple could be saved.

To any killer and every family in the world,
it is not too late for us to hope.
Our young people are the future
and if we start with them,
we can definitely make it stop.

People in America and all over the world
must say to everyone today,
"Please, Stop the Violence!"
Cause stopping the violence is the only way.

The Point of View in My Eyes

Age isn't anything but a number,
so why can't a color just be a color?
I have always said a good man is hard to find,
but it seems to me that he has come to be a different kind.

I don't view myself as prejudice
because I know I am really nice,
but when I had to let him go,
is it me or him that had to pay the price?

Why do I feel so guilty
and all so bad inside,
now there is a depression coming on
that I am desperately trying to hide.

I wish that things could be different
because I know he is probably the best person for me,
and I will never forget our little moments,
so you see.

Even though things will never work out,
he will always have a special place in my heart
and I will always care for him,
because he will always and forever be one of my best friends.

When he looks into my eyes,
and I look into his,
if it's meant for us to be together
no matter how many years go by,
we shall unite once again.

If She Only Knew

I once knew a girl
that thought she knew it all,
but she failed to realize
that one day this knowledge she had
would not last very long.

She thought she knew what love was
besides being a four letter word,
but little did she know
love was going to take a turn for the worst.

A lot of people care about her,
and even love and support what she does,
but she asked herself one question,
"Is her attitude an act from God?"

I have always heard one say
that one will be a nonbeliever,
until the day Jesus has come into their life
and it appears to be too late.

That is the day change will come,
but will it come in time?
One time a different girl
fought like cats and dogs
with her mom who knew her best.

She thought she knew it all
because "She had been there, done that."
She used profanity at her mother
and even treated her like a dog,
but later on that night
the phone rang and her mother answered.
They said, "Your baby girl is in the hospital."
Mommy jumped out of bed and went to the hospital.

She sat by her daughter's side.
The boyfriend was nowhere to be found.
God came and spoke to the daughter
and flashed what happened before her very eyes.

He said, "Honor thy mother and honor thy father,
regardless if you think you are right or wrong.
Life and death are in the power of the tongue,
and they that love it shall eat the fruit thereof."

The daughter thought about what God had said
and asked him for a second chance.
She promised that she would change
and she went through a transformation like she said.

She realized she didn't know what love was
and that she should always take it slow.
She put her mother first
because she knew that mommy knew the best way to go.

The daughter asked herself one question,
and that was, "Where in life did she want to go?"
She replied, "Graduate from high school, go to college, and allow the relationship with her mother to always prosper and grow."

Being Unique

As we grow in this society,
people are different in their own way.
We can learn from every individual.
Look at the person beside you, behind you, or in front of you
and tell them, "You are special."

It doesn't matter what color you are
or how tall or short you may be,
but one thing we must realize is that
everyone is unique.

Education is very important
to every man, woman, and child.
Never give up hope,
and go that extra mile.

Always believe in your goals
so one day you will be thankful.

Save It Until Marriage

Teenagers of our society
are trying to be more and more like adults today,
running out and having children,
even trying to start a family.

Some begin at twelve years old
and continue on and on,
not thinking clearly,
thinking having sex is not even wrong.

They think of all the enjoyment
and all the love they are going to get,
not thinking of all the consequences
of the choices they just made.

Girls are quitting school,
guys are using them for one thing,
they claim it's always love,
but then they always leave.
You have all of these diseases,
and condoms aren't 100 percent.
the only way to protect yourself is 100 percent abstinence.

The message I want to get across
 to every teenage girl around the world
is: "Sex is a special thing
that you should wait until marriage to have.
Your education is most important
because a husband or a companion will always be found out in the world."

Facing Only the Facts

As I look back to yesterday,
and the years that have passed away,
I look back to my life
and my goals along the way.

I look into my future,
wondering what lies straight ahead,
will I have what I always wanted,
Or anything I ever said?

People of our society
say you have to start out at an early age,
start with only the young
'cause only the young people can be saved.

As I enter into high school,
I must plan the rest of my life
with severe caution and excitement,
with extreme sacrifice.

One goal I have in my life
is to go to college one day.
Be what I want to be,
and be the best if I may.

I want a job at an early age
so I can work my way through school,
have the money that I want to have
and follow the golden rule.
If I want to be the best I can be,

I must start at an early age,
imagining my hopes and dreams
and making it my reality.

I realize in this community
I may not have everything that I want,
but now that I know it well
I know that truly it wasn't even my fault.

I'm only following my heart
and where it leads me to be,
nothing in this world is going to stop me,
even if it's destiny.

Mommy, You're Always Right

Growing up through my life
I was a hardheaded child.
I would never listen to my mother,
hardly ever cracked a smile.

My mommy was always right
with the words that she spoke.
It always came true,
but I took it as a joke.

I remember once upon a time
my mommy told me about my mouth.
Of course I didn't listen,
didn't even try to stop it.

I remember a long time ago
my mommy told me to stay at home.
 I went ahead anyway
and my life almost disappeared.

I never thought about death
until my life flashed before my eyes.
Sometimes I even thought,
"Why don't I commit suicide?"

I have learned one important lesson
and that is life is very sweet.
Don't say the things you would regret,
'cause it could become reality.

Mommy, you're always right
with the words that you speak,
the lessons that you have taught,
the words that you have preached.

My mommy,
I will always love you
for the things that you have done,
that special thanks I want to give
'cause you're always number 1.

Hard Decisions

As a time comes in your life
where the answer is yes or no,
where the questions are intense
and you say, "So it isn't so."

You wonder in confusion
to think and understand,
 did I make the right decision
to take it into my own hands?

Should I have asked for help,
or should I have done it alone.
The pressures that are inside me
 keep going on and on.

I think and sometimes wonder
was it a mistake,
for me to say no to the wrong things
that people go and do every day.

As a teenager
I am curious,
I want to experiment with many different things,
but as I see the world today,
saving my life is the right thing.

My advice,
as you see,
is one thing to take to mind,
say no to all the things
that will have a dramatic change over time.

What is Happiness?

Someone once asked me,
"Are you truly happy?"
I said, "Yes!"
But I had to stop and think,
"What is happiness?"

Happiness is like sunshine,
It's bright and you can see it miles away.
When you walk into a room
A light bulb will turn on instantly.

Happiness is being thankful,
Taking care of what you have,
Giving to a brother or sister who is in need,
and always brightening a room with a smile.

Happiness is finding the peace
One needs to have joy in their life.
It is accepting God as your Savior and leader
 to guide you through any situation.

Happiness is being blessed with all God has given you,
regardless of the circumstance.
It is finding the light at the end of the tunnel
for eternal happiness.

An Angel

(In memory of a beloved colleague.)

A butterfly
who spreads sunshine and happiness to all the boys and girls,
her calm voice was greater than a whisper to speak words of
encouragement to them.

She was a fierce lion
who fought any predators that surprised her on the long treacherous journey.
But no matter how rough things were,
she always would see that shining light at the end of the tunnel.

She got her boxing gloves to help her fight any battle,
while she filled her heart with ounces of hope and belief.
Her smiles were filled with happiness
because she received all the peace that she needed.

She was the rock that I found in my path
that gave me strength greater than any food.
She was the flashlight that shined the light, which guided me through
any battle or war in education I had to face.

But most of all, she will continue being a set of footprints,
that will always leave an impression on all our lives.
She was a special hero that left footprints in our hearts as well.

A Teacher Retiree

(*Dedicated to Mary Pauley, aka MOP*)

As the hot sun shines in the sky,
it's so hot that our air conditioners are on high
and we have a cup of water by our side.
Your fingers turn the pages of the calendar,
realizing that the month of August is about to begin.

You see, this August is very different and bittersweet for you.
For you are now labeled as a "teacher retiree."
The light bulb of your brain is shining brightly as you think,
"What am I going to do now?"

Your reaction,
"I don't have to go to work to decorate my classroom and see which students I will have in my class."
The Lord has blessed you with the opportunity to prosper in a different way in life.

Your eyes and brain turn into a video camera
to remember all your teaching experiences, students, colleagues, and now your empty classroom.

You close your eyes to think about all the things that retirement will bring you:
getting paid for sitting at home,
laying down on your couch, reading a book, and taking trips to any place you would like to go.

You can spend more time with your grandchildren and go to more programs at school.

You can spend more time writing your thoughts on paper, writing your manuscript to publish your first book of poetry.

In the days of your retirement, you can do the following:
Enjoy going to the beach and seeing the waves as they come near you.
Enjoy not grading papers and taking lots of paperwork home with you.
Enjoy not making copies and buzzing the office to let Terri know the copy machine is out of toner.
Enjoy relaxing during the month April instead of worrying about the infamous CRCT.

Remember having the honor of being the Hillcrest Teacher of the year during the last year of your career, but most of all, remember that you survived your teaching career and you are now officially a "teacher retiree."

Crying Unto Jesus

I cry unto you
that I touch your unchanging hand.
I have faith greater than a mustard seed,
and I know you are more powerful than any man on earth.

Father, you can do anything
as long as I come to you and ask in prayer.
You are always there for me
through the joyful times and the sins.

Lord, you know all my problems,
you know them before they come.
Sometimes I can hardly make it,
but you will always make me strong.
Yes, Jesus loves me,
this I know
for the Bible tells me so.

Jesus, I must say, "Thank you!"
and I have to say this because
Jesus is the only God I serve.
"You might not come when we want you to, but you will always be on time."

ANN B. RHODES

Facing My Reality

My eyes are tired,
ready to close,
too full of tears
to let anyone know
who I am
and what I'm for,
the problems that are inside me.

I want to share,
but I am shy,
too scared I might
let go and cry
tears of sadness,
tears of fear,
tears of hopelessness,
tears of worry.

I cannot cope
with my life today,
can't deal with the problems
from people around me
or my feelings inside,
what's going on in my life
that I desperately try to hide.

I always heard one say
about a teenager, it can be hard
having only one parent,
but still I feel ignored.

Sometimes I often wonder
and cry myself to sleep,
how I would be different
if my family was complete.

If I had a father
to guide me through the way,
to stop me when I'm doing wrong
and punish me the way I should pay.

They say a relationship with a father,
is a special, special thing.
Will I ever know
by the time I turn sixteen?

I remember I once said
I hate my father without a doubt,
but now that I have grown older
I just want to grab his neck and shout,
"Father, I love you,
for the bad things you have done.
Even though you weren't there for me, I want you with me now.
I can forgive, but I can't forget."

People of the world
must realize that
divorce or separation doesn't tear the family,
it takes the child's heart away.

ANN B. RHODES

A Mother...

A mother is a woman who shows love
as soon as her children are born into the world.
She is the person who takes care of them
and shows them all the love that they are worth.

A mother is a woman who hugs her children when they cry.
She even continues to love them
during the time they may tell a lie.

A mother is a woman
who you can call day or night.
She can advise you on any situation
so you can see the light at the end of the tunnel.

A mother is a woman
who will always be by your side.
Regardless if you are right or wrong,
she will be that motherly guide.

A mother is a woman
who will take care of you
young or old.
She has a heart full of love for everyone.
She has a heart made of gold.

A mother is a woman
who teaches her children how to read the Bible,
and how to attend church every Sunday
and that Jesus is our Savior, our Lord.

My mother is my foundation
and has always showed me the correct way to go.
She is the mother that I love,
and I am very proud to know.

About the Author

I BEGAN MY WRITING CAREER at the age of eight in the third grade. I always kept a journal to write down my thoughts. It was the inspiration from my mother and my sixth grade language arts teacher, Mrs. Kim Holstun, who encouraged me to continue writing. My first poem was published in the *Hogansville Herald* when I was in the sixth grade.

I continued writing for the school newspaper and occasionally sent poems to the *Lagrange Daily News*. During my middle school years, I wrote a poem called "Please, Stop the Violence" that was published by WSB-TV, Channel 2 Action News, in Atlanta, Georgia, in their "Please Stop the Violence" campaign. This poem was included inside school kits that were distributed to all Georgia middle schools. I had three poems, "A Great Man," "The Greatest Easter Gift," and "What is a Mother?" published in different poetry anthologies in both the United States and internationally. My poem "A Great Man" is part of a CD collection of poetry distributed by Poetry.com.

I am currently an elementary school teacher in the Troup County school system. I have a Bachelor of Arts degree in early childhood education from Lagrange College, and a master's and specialist degree in elementary education from Troy University. I still continue writing and being an inspiration to the elementary students that I teach.